Shawn M.

ROSE

LESSONS

FROM ETERNITY

University Press of the South
New Orleans

2004

Published in the United States by:
University Press of the South, Inc.
5500 Prytania Street, PMB 421
New Orleans, LA 70115 USA

E-mail: unprsouth@aol.com Fax: (504) 866-2750 Phone: (504) 866-2791
Visit our award-winning web page:
http://www.unprsouth.com
Visit our partner's web page: http://ww.punmonde.com
Acid-free paper.

Shawn M. Rose.
Lessons from Eternity.
First Edition. Poetry, 6; American Literature, 8.
x + 66 pages.

ISBN: 1-931948-36-4
Library of Congress Catalog Card Number: 2004 10 54 51

DEDICATION

Lessons from Eternity is the intellectual's call to arms. It presses for the human race to join together and to set aside our materialistic pursuits so that we may imbue our lives with truth and fulfillment. I would like to dedicate this book to all those individuals who continually invoke their creative spirit to enrich our lives both mentally and physically. Let the spiritual and intellectual evolution of a new generation begin!

table of CONTENTS

lessons from eternity

— CONTENTS —

— CONTENTS —

AUTHOR'S NOTE

Poetry elicits the raw essence of mortal emotion by charming the human spirit with each verse. The poet's vision demands introspection from the reader. It is this vision that challenges us to be more expressive, to evaluate our most sacred ideals, and to explore the very fabric that ties us all together – a common thread of personal thoughts, desires, and sentiments that makes us human. Through the words and images on the coming pages, you will enter an enchanted world fashioned from human experiences. These pages carry stories of love, of loss, and of hope – an open portal to a place where lovers dance and philosophers dream. I invite you, the reader, to share in these *Lessons from Eternity* firsthand. Welcome to my world...

ACKNOWLEDGEMENTS

Lessons from Eternity would not have been possible without the enduring patience, support, and love of several cherished people.

I greatly appreciate the efforts of my friends and colleagues at the University of Miami, who always keep me grounded. In particular, I would like to recognize Dr. Ann Flipse for always being such a strong champion of the humanities in medicine.

Many thanks to my family and friends for your unwavering support and love. Especially, to my mother, Arlene Rose, for her tutelage in the literary arts and for her endless encouragement of all my endeavors.

I would like to express my utmost gratitude to the editors and staff at the University Press of the South for your patience and for your guidance.

Lastly, a special thank you to my graphic design artist (and true love), Jamie Ng, for her inspiration, diligence, and dedication to this project, and for always making me smile.

reverie

Levitating

I sit up here on my cloud of loneliness
paying homage to the birds and sky...

awakenings

Rarely do we encounter such fleeting
moments of clarity. Mysterious and significant,
these awakenings evoke passions long forgotten.

Freedom

We are born
    and told we cannot fly

So we believe
    and cast our wings aside

Only in dreams
    does our reach exceed our grasp

While every day
    we lament our squandered past

Upon a child
    we inflict the greatest ills

We build a fence
    and impose on them our wills

We brandish words
    "impractical, impossible, absurd"

We abolish hopes
    that were striving to be heard

But heed we must
    the message left unsaid

Abandoned senses
    awaken feelings long thought dead

Our mother earth
    carries wisdom in her womb

Behind every flower
    is a bud waiting to bloom

Look to the sky
    boundless in its hues

Look to the stars
    always glimmering on cue

A lesson learned
    from masters old as time

Unafraid to aim
    for freedom of the mind

Listen to the Rain

Listen to the rain
        pavement takes a beating.
Listen to the sky
        thunderous unforgiving.
Listen to the heart
        unconditional loving.
Listen to the self
        truthful unbelieving.
Listen to the leaves
        powerless rustling.
Listen to the night
        black forgetting
to Listen to the rain.

To Be Round

Curvilinear relationships
caught between two sharpened edges.
Two extremes,
incomplete.
Somehow the middle path escapes unscathed.
If only the world was truly round
so many of us might not fall off.
The edge
stands alone,
hammered,
jaded,
to a perfect point.
While those in the middle slide along
coming full circle to completion.
Ah,
to be round.

Myself

Sometimes I see a picture
hanging on the wall.
It burns an image
deep inside,
straight through to the soul.

The paper calls out to me,
craving for some ink.
I resist its tempting glances,
choosing not to think.

My God,
what if they see
a piece of me?
Something that escapes format.

Confined behind the lens,
a distorted image that pretends
to be reality.

Trapped in body.
Encased in flesh.
Never able to express,
or love and feel,
without pangs of guilt.

Why not love thyself?
Why not cherish thyself?
Why not worship thyself?

O what a foolish notion
that God is man
and man is God.
But still you ache
for mother's womb,

that watery tomb
from which you've
been set free.

I beg to differ.
I've never felt stiffer
here in this casket.

Ashes to ashes
and dust to dust.
The only thing I trust
is that I'll die someday.

But what about those
who are already dead?
Instead, I choose to live.

Do not sleepwalk through the day.
Try to find a way
to breathe life and plant a seed
so that all of humanity
will have a chance to embrace
and have a taste
of true immortalilty.

But why should I
give to mankind
the secret of all time?

Lock it up
and throw away the key.
And they will never know
that all along
it was me.

Truth

Ever since that incipient breath,
I opened up my eyes
and took in the world.
The *tabula rasa,*
naïve and free.

At my inception
the black veil descended,
draping my sight.
I was afraid for the first time
because I knew that I had lost you.

And so my journey began...
so very long ago.
I have spent my entire life searching,
leaving no stone unturned
and no blanket uncovered.

I have scanned the horizon
only to catch fleeting glimpses
of your wholeness and purity.

When it seems that I have finally found you,
you slip right through my fingers
like timeless grains of hourglass sand.

Each moment passes,
like whispered childhood promises,
and still I seek your succor.

I have traveled to far-off lands
and tasted exotic spices.
You were not there.

I have roamed the ancient ruins
and perused the works of scholars.
You were not there.

I have knelt before altars
and prayed to idol gods.
You were not there.

I have searched the heavens
and explored distant moons.
You were not there.

I have scrutinized, compartmentalized,
and dissected the natural element.
Still, you were not there.

Am I doomed to live forever in your shadow?

In wealth, in power, in achievement –
innumerable veils have shrouded my vision.

I keep on crawling out of this ditch
that has devoured me since birth,
while you shovel dirt onto my head
and drive me deeper into the abyss.

My strength is replenished
by the fountains of knowledge
that I choose to pursue.

When I cannot go on any longer,
once more, I open up my eyes
and peer into the mirror.

I am found.
We are one and the same –
you and I.

You were with me all along –
the truth.

An Artist's Vision

There is something in the eyes of an artist...
An intensity sculpted through years of turmoil.

His soul is sprawled before the critic's pen.
Yet, his genius is unfettered by its lashes.

Our norms are dull and frivolous –
His lone obligation is to create.

His medium, a spectrum of emotion.
His canvas, a panegyric to mankind.

Amorphous borders form, and dark meets light.
They are one and the same.

Reality is a facade, obscured by perception.
To this, his eyes are a testament.

ablaze

Lion's Whisper

Inside you is a lion's roar
dulled to the whisper of a cat's meow.

Your eyes speak in metaphors
of dreams not yet dreamt,
kept locked away in a hidden vault
amongst other forgotten treasures.

The light is on in the attic,
but no one is home to respond
to the buzz, buzz, buzzing
of subconcious impulses
flittering inside your skull.

Your virtues have become weapons,
forcibly maintaining a barrier
between the real and the sublime.

You are afraid,
always reaching out to test the water
when it is so much easier to dive right in.

You like things sugarcoated,
but with the first sign of bitterness
you roll it around on your tongue
and spit it out.

You are missing the point.
Forget raging storms,
for without dull gray skies
by what standard can we measure our precious sun?

Transformation comes in little pieces,
like the first snowflake of winter
that flutters helplessly toward the scorching earth,
paving the way for the changing of the season.

The tide has turned.
It is time to march to the beat of a different drummer.
Listen.
Do you hear it?

It is the sound of your own heart.
Or have you forgotten?

Daytime Dreamer

Do you ever dream while you are awake?
Dip into streaming subconcious...

Set free strung pearls of wisdom
Casting shadows on inhibition
Reach down inside and envision

Knotted dogma taken out
Smashing mirrors of self-doubt
Credence free to dance about

Empty canyons fill with tears
Stifled child through the years
No longer subject to its fears

Airing word after word that slices
A deaf ear to mankind's vices
Tasting latent, foreign spices

Do you ever dream while you are awake?
Ride a wave on the unknown...

Dry impulse given form
Breaking free of every norm
Strong, refusing to conform

At the mercy of a whim
Aching from limb to limb
Mind pours forth a lyric hymn

Paints a portrait of the soul
Complement to every whole
Gilded genius in the skull

Quakes with vision indescript
Tepid fibers rightly stripped
Former masters being whipped

Do you ever dream while you are awake?
Sail the earth until its end...

Entertain the heart's desire
Fuel the burning fire
Never does it tire

Only grows and multiplies
In the blink of an eye
Beyond the limits of the sky

Unleash the beast within
Deceased for no one's sin
Creativity begins

Calls upon no other
Neither sister, son, nor brother
This freedom has no mother

Do you ever dream while you are awake?
Levitate on H_2O...

To walk on shattered glass
Sharp mind, with a single pass
Cuts through solid mass

Prometheus unbound
Concrete spool unwound
Devoid of any sound

Glide like eagles in the breeze
Ignorant to all disease
Brings me to my knees

Thunderclaps of inspiration
Release the imagination
Behold my proclamation

Do you ever dream while you are awake?
I do.

awaken

Dancing to the rhythm of another.
Floating through the day, intoxicated with love.
Sustained by those we hold dear.

The Temptress

The temptress beckons...
The scented oils of her skin
burn like incense in my nares.

The temptress beckons...
Our bodies drenched in sweat,
saturating lovers' scent.

The temptress beckons...
Her nectar whets my thirst
like a spring tinged with honey.

The temptress beckons...
My day is filled with promise
of another evening by her side.

The temptress beckons...
She weaves a web around my heart
with jet-black threads of silken hair.

The temptress beckons...
I would not care to live
but for one last caress.

The temptress beckons...
Our love is like Apollo's rays,
ablaze with fierce desire.

The temptress beckons...
With lids drawn tightly shut,
we sense its warm red flame.

The temptress beckons...
As I play amidst the moon and stars,
she dances in my subconscious.

The temptress beckons...
Even in slumber I am her slave,
tilling dreams with efflorescence.

The temptress beckons...
Like beacons in the passing night,
her eyes cede passage to the soul.

The temptress beckons...
With first light, I awaken,
and behold her glowing face.

The temptress beckons...
She softly chants a morning tune,
welcoming the day anew.

The temptress beckons...
Her song tells of a champion
conquered only by her love.

The temptress beckons...
I long to fill that lover's shoes,
prepared at last to give myself.

The temptress beckons...
And I heed her lulling call.

The Blink

Her eyes are closed.
She does not even know
that I exist,
or that I study her form
with an artist's zeal.
Her every curve
and every crease
are tattooed memories
upon the canvas in my mind.
How can she know
my heart's desire
if her eyelids
are so tightly drawn?
Does she dream
of life with me,
as I with her,
when sleep dust settles
in the eve?

Her eyes are half-closed.
White blankets melt
into crescent seas of blue.
She peers through downcast lids
that shade her from
the piercing sun.
A hidden observer
of her radiance,
I take care
to go unnoticed.
My conscience aches
to spill forth
ages of repressed passion.

Does she know
  that I would sail the earth
  unto its end
  to bathe a minute
  in her virgin waters?

Her eyes are opened.
  Like sparkling sapphires,
  their sheen dances off
  wavebreaks of aquamarine.
The blackness
  of their apertures
  absorbs the scene
  before her.
My heart escapes rhythm
  as our eyes embrace.
  I am frozen
  in her gaze,
  and for a fleeting instant,
  the hands of time
  take respite.
She knows I am a slave,
  bonded faithfully
  by an enduring love.

Dearly Belusted

her lips slightly parted
blow me a kiss
her arms draw me closer
in sweet, tender bliss

her eyes shine right through me
hidden desire revealed
her thighs stand before me
beckoning layers unpeeled

her tongue whets my thirst
glides across scented skin
her ears detect sounds
of delightful proportion

her breast heaving rhythm
breathes for us both
her mouth tastes like candy
enveloping my growth

her neck white as milk
marked by our lust
her back torn to shreds
with each mighty thrust

her loins hold a secret
like a virgin kept fresh
her body deluges me
with pleasures of the flesh

Forbidden

Sweet kiss.
Soft,
Silky,
Cheek's caress.
Unleashing primal desire.
White garb,
A virgin's dress.
Heartthrobs escape the mire.
Like an angel you descend.
Pure intention,
Disguised as lust.
Bohemian tastes offend,
Disrobing temptation's thrust.

I hold you in my hand

Take no notice
Pass me by
Beauty is in the eye
Of the beholder
So they say

I lost my heart
I lost my mind
In your opaque windows
To the soul

I cannot find
An inner peace
That will last eternally
Let me be
Struggling to breathe

Sweet embrace
Soft caress
Carefully undress
The great facade

Stop the lie
You must give in
Close your eyes
I'll open my heart

For you to treasure
And to hold
Never let it go
The dream remains untold

I hold it in my hand
The universe unwound
And I will share
A piece of it with you

Goddess

When your lips touch mine
a thousand worlds collide
and crash against the sun.

A new galaxy is born.
It draws my heart into a storm
and commands me to your side.

The wind whispers your name.
Mirrors echo your gentle frame.
Your smile lights the skies above.

I long to fill your sweet embrace
and take you to that place
where lovers dance in ecstasy.

If angels had no wings,
you would exemplify those things
that only Heaven can endure.

I pledge to you my soul.
Together we are whole.
You are my Goddess.
I am your God.

The Pledge

Your weight upon my chest
Your warmth beside my own
Your breath upon my cheek
Your scent within my room

I rest quietly, saturated by your essence
Primed to burst into the day
Seizing you fully
As our differences melt away

A tender embrace
Molds a union of our souls
Gracefully, you dance through my thoughts
And monopolize my dreams

Your spell has been cast
I am but a helpless fool
Captivated by your movements
Entranced by your sweet song

I dream of waterfalls and mists
Our naked bodies basking in the sun
Waves crashing against our skin
As we soak in each other's rays

I am released within you
As we perform the lover's dance
Our hearts rejoice in splendor
Illuminating the shadows of my life

What is dull and ordinary
Becomes florid by your side
I blindly risk the tightrope trail
Without a safety net below

With the knowledge that
You will always break my fall
For this alone –
I pledge to you my love

Powerless

Your body is a temple
whose walls I have known before.
When inside,
I hear the ancestral calling
and I am liberated.

I know not from where
comes the familiarity of your touch.
But with every breath,
I breathe for you.

Your eyes hold me captive.
My freedom I would surely give
to catch a glimpse of your
womanhood in all its splendor.

Like the softening of winter's blanket,
I melt before you.
With a drop of your sweet, feminine nectar,
I am transformed
into a suckling child
whose mother's milk
sustains him outside the womb.

From your tree of life,
I pluck a twig.
It grows into a forest.
At once I am lost and strangely found,
running circles through the foliage
while guided by your radiance.

You grasp my naked hand
and draw me back into your temple.
I drink from your holy spring
and bathe in the waters of redemption.

I am forbidden.
I am forgiven.
I am powerless.

Gratitude

To my father, I owe the mountains –
His foundation never crumbled
Beneath the burden of a home.

To my mother, I owe the oceans –
Ages ago, I drowned in cardiac lullabies
Within her inviting cradle.

To my child, I owe the sun –
I am renewed by his innocence,
Forever basking in his brilliance.

To myself, I owe the thunder –
The roaring spirit within
Who is never dampened by the rain.

To my Lord, I owe the world –
Who has given me the hands
To build a heaven here on earth.

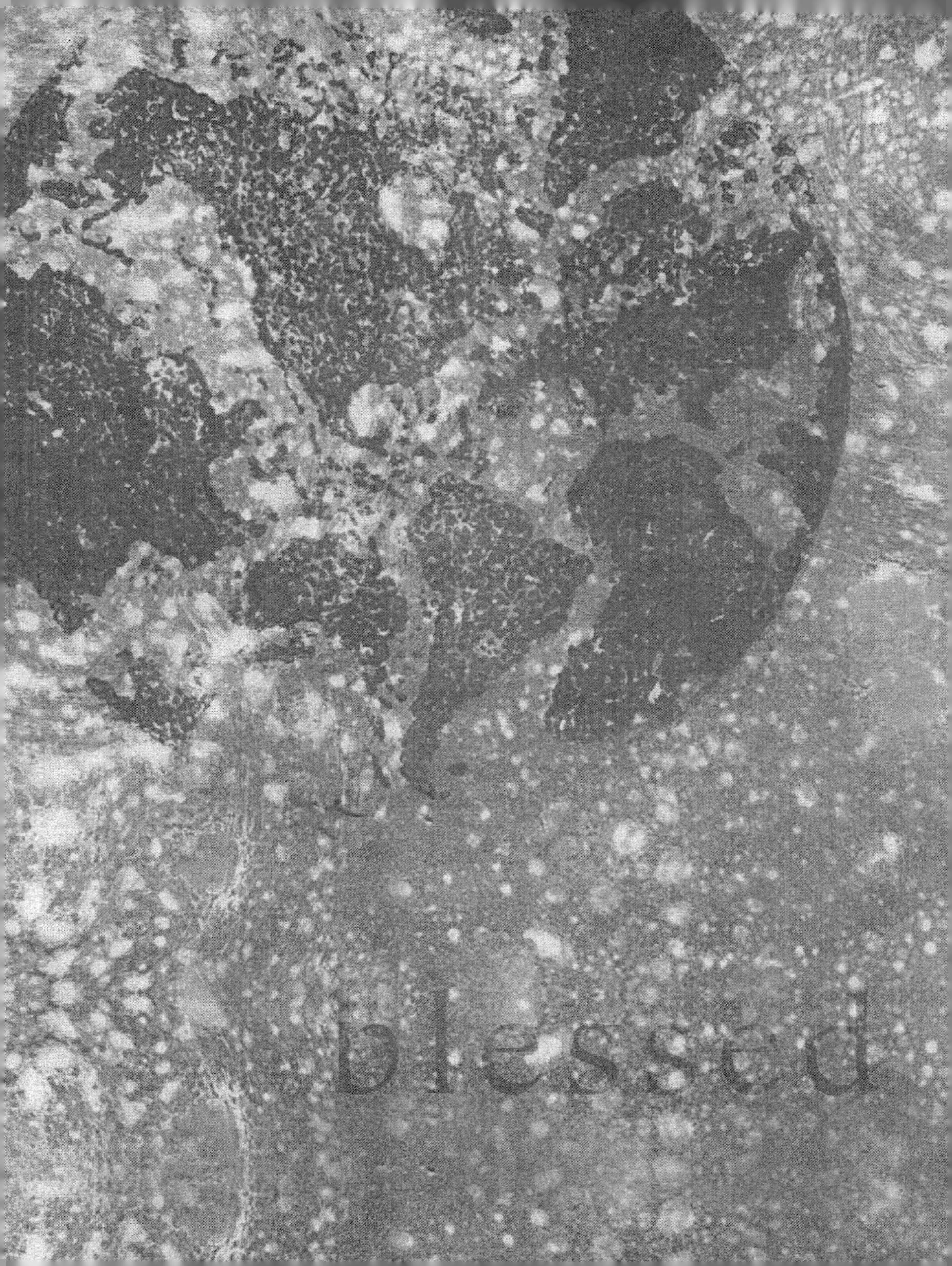
blessed

portraits of Mankind

Glimpses through the living room window.
A spectrum of human experience.
Mirroring our most glorious achievements
and our greatest shortcomings.

Middletown America

Middletown America –
        the only true poetry.
Middletown America –
        someplace to live,
        someplace to be.

Bricklayer's paradise
or gardener's dream,
with sweet aroma
of lilac in the air
and dandelion pollen
carried by the stream.

Sunday afternoon barbecues ablaze –
burgers seared
to plump sheer delight,
barking dogs and children's squints
at summer's glaze.

Playfully giggling,
running through sprinkler baths,
sitting on father's lap,
steering the old Chevy
on evening drives.

As families gather for mealtime,
ritualistic laughs
preserve generations past
with the waxed finish
of days long gone.

Grandmothers rocking,
mothers tending dishes,
children hunting snipe,
fathers and sons play catch,
chasing baseballs
destined for neighbors' lawns.

Ah yes, the suburbs –
Porches filled with smiling faces.
Memories of weekday worries
smoked away
in father's evening pipe.

Darkness falls and porch lights dim,
glittering specks
across nighttime skies.
This is happiness.
This is bliss.
A portrait safe from critics' eyes.

The stale night air caresses
golden, combed strands.
Flags flap gently,
kissing the breeze
with nationalistic dignity.

In bed, wives draw closer,
extracting warmth
from tired hands.

Middletown America –
        the only true poetry.
        Like clockwork...
Middletown America –
        someplace to live,
        someplace to be.

Jazzy

Saxophones squeal in smooth harmony
like lovers' lingo lulling the soft caress
of music across ashen asphalt.

An entourage of city lights
sent blissfully to sleep
by silky songs of slick jazziness.

Bounding tunes
break silent cityscapes,
piercing the somber skyline.

Reverberations of musical tranquility
send me soaring to spiritual heights
as I reciprocate its sweet embrace.

Nightly notes fill teaspoons
of fuel for poetry, all tucked away
in suave nocturnal symphony.

Who can but wonder why musicians sleep
so soundly after splaying their souls
across score-filled pages?

An artist's slate is bare no more
as he delicately drums on the canvas floor
while splattering his strokes in haphazard hues.

Vocalists weave words
into webs of intrigue,
filling symphonic volumes of wisdom.

A telling tribute to rooftop warriors
whose vision wisps us
into somnolent serenity...

Street Warrior

While enlisted men chase terrorists
through desert dunes,
the street warrior battles hunger
on the homefront.

Disease, exposure, and isolation
are his daily horrors.
For he is the forgotten warrior
who served his country proudly
many ages ago...

He bathes in infested waters
and sleeps on a concrete mattress.
Camouflaged into the earth,
fatigue now bears new meaning.

He desperately tries to collect
the remnants of a shattered mind.
His return to normalcy,
the impossible dream,
mind-numbing,
bending, bowing, breaking...

Incessant longing for an identity,
for a place to call his own –
as the sands of time collect
in a steady, enduring mound.

He is a nameless face,
amidst a sea of crowded urbanites.
He chooses anonymity,
rather than face indignity
or remembrance of times long gone.

A new generation of warriors
is being shaped at present.
Surrounded by death and chaos,
they lose a piece of their humanity
with each cannon blast –

Who will save the street warriors of tomorrow?

The Epidemic

A society unkempt.
Laid to ruins by the terrible virus
that swept across the land,
filling mind after impressionable young mind
with hatred and intolerance.

Those infected became possessed
by greed and lust
for absolute sovereignty.
Their progeny were cultured in plastic pods
lined with dollar bills.
Fistfuls of illusionary currency
was all it took
to launch an all-out war
on the art of reason.

Institutions of learning
were among the first to succumb.
Government and commerce
were condemned long ago.
Then science.
Then religion.

And art, so pristine,
held upon the pedestal of mankind
since the infancy of civilization,
should surely be immune.

But, art too has fallen victim.

Perhaps Darwin never realized that
evolution can indeed proceed in reverse.

The Western Wall

I hear a voice.
It speaks of a nation everlasting.
She cries into the wind for peace.

The worshippers exalt her.
Stone-faced, they stand before the wall.
Tears drape their solemn faces.
Their beards are soaked in blood
from years of suffering and slaughter.

As I stand beneath the curtain of her shadow,
I weep for joy.

The mighty shofar blasts.
Its vibrations are my essence.
The ancient chants echo in unison below.

I gaze upon the sky
and embrace the sunset, moon, and stars:
Their brilliance wanes
before the sentinel above
that bears the Star of David.

Something wonderful

I saw something today –
Something wonderful.
It brought me hope.
Perhaps there is a future for humanity!

A haggard man,
A soldier,
All too forgotten,
Makes his home near my own.

An old bus stop,
Abandoned by drivers long ago.
A tattered sheet blankets the ground,
His bed.

A cotton rag engulfs his scraggly hair.
He is a man of faith.
His shirt, stained from years of street life,
Drapes a single arm.

But he does not beg,
Nor does he complain.
He lies down on the pavement.
It is his home.

A stranger, a wanderer,
Passes by.
The stranger halts abruptly.
He has forgotten something.

From his pocket,
The stranger draws a plastic bag.
The man's eyes are hungry with anticipation.
What surprise does the bag conceal?

The stranger unfolds the bag
And smoothes out the creases.
And behold,
A piece of fruit it bears.

He gives it to the tired soldier
And moves along his way.
On this day,
The man will eat.

Sweet nectar,
Like rain,
Will trickle down his throat,
Refreshing his barren gut.

He has received the gift of sustenance
From someone who had nothing else to give.
He may yet survive another day,
And so shall we.

Moondancer

Soft shadows slink at nightfall
tracing silhouettes of evening dwellers
concealed within the brush.

The buzz of the cicadas
echoes sweet cricket melodies
immersed in nocturnal symphony.

From distant dwellings right on cue
the canine chorus strikes a chord
professing love to the waning moon.

Palm trees sway in the cool night breeze
weaving wistfully in unison
with lapping waves of river drums.

Leaves rustle in the naked streets
as stoplights flash their hypnotic hues
upon the charcoaled asphalt.

In the silence and the blackness
most slip off into the abyss
of somnolent tranquility.

While the city sleeps I dance
in the ecstasy of Diana's rays
entranced by the evening song.

ecstasy

ending

Birth. Embracing the drum of mother's womb.
Death. Cessation of existence in the finite realm.
Ending or Beginning?

Oblivion

These words are screaming
to be unleashed
as I stare blankly
at the empty page.

Thoughts of you
haunt me
and make me
your slave.

I embark on a sojourn
to a place
where angels dance
to the trumpeting
of Gabriel's horn –
bringing me ever closer
to Heaven's door.

The sentinels of serenity
glance about surreptitiously,
daring to take the plunge
as the lightkeeper flashes
for their safe passage.

The breeze speaks in whispers,
extinguishing torches
with its tender breath.

Stargazers scan the horizon,
trying to catch a glimpse
of infinity –
where captainless ships
sail into the unknown.

Time stands still,
knowing neither beginning nor end,
but tries desperately,
nonetheless,
to leave a footprint in the sand.

The muses lay waiting
by the gates of oblivion,
casting spells with their song,
absolving poor souls
once born a blank slate
who now return home.

Aged

Restless youth turned ashen gray,
creeping,
ever so slowly,
through the gates of silence.

Blackness surrounds
as memories fade into the mist.
What was consciousness
becomes tangled in
the web of forgetfulness.

Senility for all.
Sublimity for some.
Justice for none.

But reach they may
for a time come and gone
of skipping rocks off
the water by the seashore,
or flying kites
in the gentle autumn breeze.

Whisked up high,
failed control,
dipping and diving,
ever deeper into the unknown.

Abandoned by reason,
by dignity,
by pride.

Each crease
a fold of wisdom –
mistaken for a sign of decay.

Each story
a piece of time –
never to be duplicated.
Chapters closed forever,
never to be turned again.

Each smile
a cry for help –
to be nurtured,
to be remembered,
to be loved.

Yet, largely ignored
by those who haven't
the time or the patience,
by those whose diapers
have once been changed,
but now all grown up,
forget from whence they came.

And so they remain
a shadow of their former selves.
Cast aside into humility
to be forever
humming softly,
by themselves,
to hide the pain.

Entangled

Spider's web, so dense, so cold
intricately spun from angel's gold.
Trapped within the threads,
no way to move.
Your venom seeps into my vein
like a thousand needles sewing sins
into my helpless, aching soul.
Unable to scream.
Unable to run.
I'll call it the paradox,
the unachievable.
It is the one you'll never grasp.

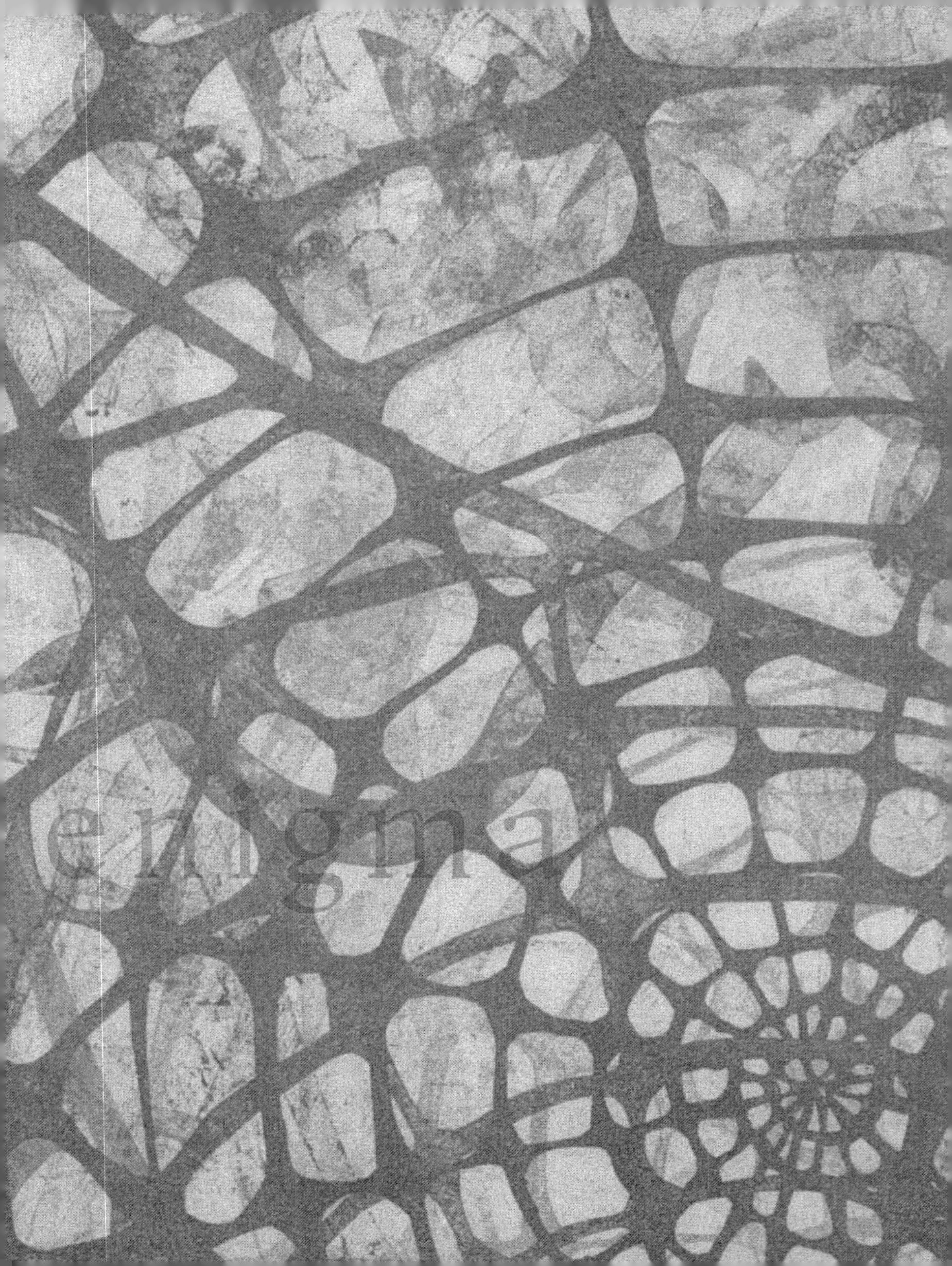
enigma

Lifeless

Gentle thunderclap
kissed the shivering, moonlit sky.
Distant clouds of mist whisked by
as the headlights waxed and waned
amidst the rolling foothills.

I sat there peering
through the living room window,
hypnotized by the steady
tap, tap, tapping
of raindrops against the glass.

Then came a horrific silence
that foreshadowed disaster.
Like the shriek of a thirsting vampire bat,
the braking cry of automobiles
pierced the still landscape.

Her lifeless body
lay unnaturally contorted
upon the crimson asphalt.

As she bled,
I bled.
Oddly, I held my breath –
trying to identify
with the stillness of her breast.

Suicide

Slight of hand,
shadows fall,
as she gives the revolver head.

Cursed mistakes,
vanishing dreams,
broken promises.

And with the black of night,
her innocence ends.

Instance

An image cast upon the screen
catching glimpses of a dream.
Father Time stands idly by.
Tick-Tock.
Tick-Tock.
Rhythmic droning of the hour hand
lays siege onto the minute,
never looking back.
Progress necessitates
a unidirectional plunge into the now.
What has passed with
the blink of an eyelash
becomes solidified in pictures of an age.
Amorphous figurines spinning
concentric rings around
the quadrangular template
for future generations to unfold.
Dissect.
Analyze.
Compartmentalize.
Every second.
Every verse.
Until all that is left
is a fragmented vision
of what could have been.

fleeting

Eulogy

Do not fear for I am near –
I am here and there
and everywhere.

Whose kingdom comes to a close at dusk
while hammered nails enclose my breast
through rusted iron gates I rest...

Newly dug pitch settled moist,
no bodily warmth, no single voice
with still, cool air remains a choice...

That I may live forever more
in the minds of men and their folklore
should I return from Heaven's door...

Let the angels sing and praise my name
and spring to life my encumbered frame
or return to dust from whence I came...

With severed cord from Mother Earth
left behind purged mortal worth
to start afresh a second birth...

And lend my soul to skies above
as freedom rolls on wings of doves
to sun and moon, profess my love...

And follow Icarus's lead,
but should thy comfort be in need,
cry to the wind, the call I'll heed...

Do not fear for I am near –
I am here and there
and everywhere.

Peace at Last

The most beautiful thing
I have ever seen...

Burden of one final breath.
Uplifted spirit, free to roam.
Weighted consciousness
into the great unknown.

Still breast
and shaded eyes.
Cold, clammy skin
with purplish tint.

An enduring image
of pain undone,
suffering gone,
Peace at last.